Who Lives in a Colorful Coral Reef?

Rachel Lynette

PowerKiDS press

New York

To Dewayne who can identify all the reef fish

Published in 2011 by The Rosen Publishing Group, Inc.
29 East 21st Street, New York, NY 10010

First Edition

Editor: Joanne Randolph
Book Design: Greg Tucker
Photo Researcher: Jessica Gerweck

Photo Credits: Cover, pp. 5 (top), 5 (bottom), 6–7, 8, 9, 11 (top), 11 (bottom), 12, 13, 15, 18–19, 21 Shutterstock.com; p. 4 © www.iStockphoto.com/Adrian Baddeley; p. 10 Jeff Rotman/Getty Images; p. 14 © www.iStockphoto.com/Grźegorz Choinski; pp. 16–17 © Norbert Probst/age fotostock; p. 20 Alexander Safonov/Getty Images; p. 21 © Ton Koene/age fotostock.

Library of Congress Cataloging-in-Publication Data

Lynette, Rachel.
  Who lives in a colorful coral reef? / Rachel Lynette. — 1st ed.
      p. cm. — (Exploring habitats)
  Includes index.
  ISBN 978-1-4488-0677-5 (library binding) — ISBN 978-1-4488-1281-3 (pbk.) — ISBN 978-1-4488-1282-0 (6-pack)
  1. Coral reef animals—Juvenile literature. I. Title.
  QL125.M55 2011
  591.77'89—dc22

                                      2009054350

Manufactured in the United States of America

CPSIA Compliance Information: Batch #WS10PK: For Further Information contact Rosen Publishing, New York, New York at 1-800-237-9932

Contents

What Is Coral?

Have you ever seen a piece of coral? A piece of coral may look like a rock, but it is really made from the skeletons of dead animals! Small animals called coral polyps live together in **colonies**.

Not all corals build reefs. Cup corals, such as these, do not build reefs. They may grow in warm or cold water. Here you can see them trying to catch food with their many arms.

Polyps have soft bodies. There are many different kinds of coral. They use **tentacles** to catch tiny bits of food floating in the water. Polyps build hard skeletons around themselves to keep their soft bodies safe.

Coral polyps grow in many different shapes, colors, and sizes. These polyps have a branching shape.

When polyps die, they leave their skeletons behind. More polyps live and then die on top of these skeletons. Over many years, the skeletons make coral reefs.

Do you see how the shape and color of this colony of coral polyps differs from the others on this page?

What Is a Coral Reef?

Sometimes many colonies of polyps grow close together. As they live and die, their skeletons build up. After a long time, large, rocky places called coral reefs form. Some of the biggest coral reefs are thousands of years old.

Here you can see a busy and colorful coral reef. Thousands of fish swim among corals, sponges, and more.

A coral reef is full of life! More animals live on or near coral reefs than in any other part of the ocean. It is not uncommon for one reef to have hundreds of snail **species**, 60 different kinds of corals, and several hundred species of fish in it.

Some fish and other animals eat coral polyps. Other fish come to the reef to eat those fish. Many animals, including baby fish, use the small holes and openings in a reef to hide from **predators**.

Stuck on You

Some animals make their homes on a reef and never leave it. Live polyps, sea anemones, and sponges fix themselves to the reef. Sea anemones look like large polyps. They can be brightly colored,

Brown tube sponges pull water in through the holes in their body walls. They take food and oxygen from the water and then push it out through the top of the tube.

but watch out. Their tentacles are **poisonous**!

Sponges are very simple animals. They do not have any **organs**, such as a brain or a heart. Sponges eat with their whole bodies! Water flows through

tiny holes all over the sponge's body. The sponge eats the tiny bits of food that float in with the water. Sponges can be smaller than your fist or several times bigger than you are!

Sea anemones, like this one, fix themselves to the reef. There are more than 1,000 different kinds of sea anemones.

Colorful sea stars, sea urchins, and sea cucumbers may not look alike, but they are all echinoderms. Most echinoderms are round, with five **symmetrical** parts. They have many tiny feet with suckers on them to help the animals move.

"Echinoderm" means "spiny skinned." It is easy to see why when you look at this red sea urchin.

As many reef animals do, sea stars eat sponges, clams, mussels, and coral polyps. They eat these animals in an unexpected way, though. Sea stars eat by pushing their stomachs out through their mouths! First a hunting sea star

There are 2,000 kinds of sea stars. Sea stars do not have brains or blood. They have been known to grow new arms or even nearly whole new bodies, if needed.

would cover its **prey** with its stomach. The **digestive juices** from its stomach then make the prey into **liquid**. In the end, the sea star sucks its stomach and the prey back into its body.

Sea cucumbers can be anywhere from .75 inch to 6 feet (2–200 cm) long. They move and eat using many tiny tube feet.

From Shellfish to Squid

Echinoderms are not the only small animals living and hunting on or near reefs. Crustaceans, such as crabs, shrimp, and lobsters, make their homes in holes in reefs.

Both squid and octopuses, like the one shown here, are predators. They use their long arms to catch their prey.

They may also hide themselves under the sand at the base of reefs.
Mollusks, such as clams, mussels, and oysters, live in the reef habitat, too. These shellfish attach themselves to the reef or hide in the sand.

Did you know that squid and octopuses are mollusks, too? It is true. Their shells are smaller and inside their bodies, though. Octopuses hide in reef caves. Squid swim around the reef in small schools.

Cleaner shrimp are one kind of crustacean that lives in a coral reef. They are called cleaner shrimp because they eat harmful animals living on reef fish.

Plenty of Fish in the Sea

Fish are everywhere on a coral reef! In fact, more than 4,000 kinds of fish swim around coral reefs. Small damselfish swim quickly in and out of the coral. Damselfish fearlessly chase away much larger parrot fish.

Beautiful butterfly fish fool predators with markings that look like eyes near their tails. Predators attack their tails, making it easier for the butterfly fish to escape.

Parrot fish come to the reef to eat **algae** growing on the coral with their beaklike mouths.

Clown fish and sea anemones have a special partnership, called a **symbiotic relationship**. Colorful clown fish hide from predators among the sea anemones. The clown fish help the anemones by cleaning algae and other matter from the anemone's skin.

Sea anemones have a deadly sting, but clown fish have a coating on their skin that keeps them safe.

Dinnertime at the Reef

The reef is like an all-you-can-eat snack bar for predators. Sharks and rays come to the reef to hunt the plentiful animals.

Rays spend most of their time near the ocean floor. They eat animals that are

The nurse shark hunts the reef at night. It eats fish, mollusks, and even corals. It likes stingrays the best.

hiding on the seabed. They find them by smell and by using another sense. This other sense lets rays feel the tiny **electric charges** given off by hidden animals.

Sharks hunt using these two senses, too. Many reef sharks are small, but blacktip sharks can be 5 feet (1.5 m) long. These fierce predators hunt in groups.

Fast-Swimming Sea Turtles

Most sea turtles live in the open ocean and come to the reef to find a quick meal. Sea turtles are excellent swimmers. They can travel up to 35 miles per hour (56 km/h)! That is about half as fast as your car generally travels on a freeway.

There are seven kinds of sea turtles swimming in Earth's oceans. This hawksbill turtle hunts for sponges.

Sea turtles spend most of their time under water, but they must come to the top to breathe. Turtles have lungs, as people do, not gills, which fish have.

When they are awake, they come up to the top every few minutes to breathe. When they are sleeping, though, they can stay underwater for over 2 hours!

Giants of the Reef

Like sea turtles, dolphins and whales spend most of their time in open water and come to the reef to eat. Spinner dolphins eat fish and squid in the deeper parts of the reef.

Humpback whales, such as this baby whale, come to the reef in the winter to feed on krill. Both dolphins and whales live in groups, called pods.

One of the biggest visitors to the coral reef is the humpback whale. It can be up to 50 feet (15 m) long and weigh up to 40 tons (36 t)! Although these whales are very big, they eat only tiny sea animals called krill and small fish. Humpback whales spend only the winter months at the reef. During the spring, they swim thousands of miles (km) to the cold water near Alaska.

These two dolphins swim in the reefs off of Tuvalu, a group of islands in the South Pacific Ocean.

Caring for the Coral Reefs

Sometimes people do things that hurt coral reefs. Fishing can take away too many fish from the reef. **Pollution** is another big problem for coral reefs. Coral polyps and other ocean animals cannot live in polluted waters.

We do not want to lose coral reefs. They are home to so many different kinds of beautiful and colorful life, such as this red sponge.

Without polyps there can be no reefs! It is important for people to take care of coral reefs. We must be careful when we boat or swim near them. The thousands of animals that live there are counting on us!

Glossary

algae (AL-jee) Plantlike living things that live in water.

colonies (KAH-luh-neez) Groups that live together.

digestive juices (dy-JES-tiv JOOS-ez) Matter in the body that helps break down food into energy.

electric charges (ih-LEK-trik CHAHRJ-ez) Power that can produce light, heat, or movement.

liquid (LIH-kwed) Matter that flows.

organs (AWR-gunz) Parts inside the body that do jobs.

poisonous (POYZ-nus) Causing pain or death.

pollution (puh-LOO-shun) Manmade wastes that hurt Earth.

predators (PREH-duh-terz) Animals that kill other animals for food.

prey (PRAY) An animal that is hunted by another animal for food.

species (SPEE-sheez) One kind of living thing.

symbiotic relationship (sim-bee-O-tik rih-LAY-shun-ship) A connection between two living things in which they help each other live.

symmetrical (sih-MEH-trih-kul) Describes an object that is the same on both sides.

tentacles (TEN-tih-kulz) Long, thin growths on animals that are used to touch, hold, or move.

Index

Web Sites

Due to the changing nature of Internet links, PowerKids Press has developed an online list of Web sites related to the subject of this book. This site is updated regularly. Please use this link to access the list:
www.powerkidslinks.com/explore/ccr/